Literature written for young adults...

by young adults.

Allow yourself to be surprised.

The Divine Line

Young Writers Chapbook Series

Jacobi Copeland

VERBALEYZE **Press**

Atlanta

Cover artwork © 2013 by Susan Arauz Barnes
Editing by Derek Koehl and Tavares Stephens
ISBN: 978-0-9856451-4-4

VerbalEyze Press books are available at special discounts for bulk purchases in the United States by corporations, institutions and other organizations.

For information, address VerbalEyze Press, 1376 Fairbanks Street SW, Atlanta, Georgia 30310.

VerbalEyze does not participate, endorse, or have any authority or responsibility concerning private correspondence between our authors and the public. All mail addressed to authors are forwarded, but the publisher cannot, unless specifically instructed by the author, give out an address or phone number.

VerbalEyze Press
A division of VerbalEyze, Inc.
www.verbaleyze.org

Jacobi wants to dedicate his first book of poems to his sister, Maya, and his parents, Carlos and Tanisha.

They support his love of language by listening to his poetry, and Jacobi believes that their feedback helps him improve his work.

Table of Contents

The Divine Line

Foreword

Many a black and white speckled notebook has been privy to the growing pains of young artists. They sketch, narrate, poet and rhyme to make sense of the world and orient themselves to the gravitational pull of coming of age. But their musings beg for answers and an empathetic head nod, so Ya-Heard? Poetics was born.

Whether speaking heartache at the mic, spitting social commentary over tracks or texting observations into the ether, the power and influence of word is undeniable and YaHeard? Poets study the craft, explore their creative process and learn how to promote their artistic endeavors through collaborations with organizations like VerbalEyze, a beacon for young artists.

YaHeard? was founded by Educator-Artists to support the creative stirrings of tweens and teens and the publication of this chapbook honors and encourages the work of a young artists whose passion and talent confirms them as part of a new generation of prolific writers, artists and musicians. Their musings have escaped from first notebooks and into your hands. Answer if you dare; head nod if you must ---this young scribe dares to explore the power of voice.

Ya Heard?

Susan Arauz Barnes
Co-founder, YaHeard? Poetics

Editors' Note

The Young Writers Chapbook Series is an expression of the mission and vision that is core to what we do at VerbalEyze. Through this series, we are able to provide talented, emerging young authors their debut introduction to the reading public. We are grateful that you also share an enthusiasm for young authors and the vibrant and energized perspectives they bring to our shared understanding of the human experience and what it means to live, love, long, lose and wonder as we travel together through this world.

We are pleased to bring to you an exceptional young writer, Jacobi Copeland, with this edition of the Young Writers Chapbook series. We trust that you will be as engaged and challenged by her words as we have been. Jacobi is part of an exceptional group of young writers, YaHeard? Poetics. He and his fellow writers are an never-ending encouragement and inspiration to us.

Read, enjoy and, as always, *allow yourself to be surprised*.

Derek Koehl
Tavares Stephens

Full Clouds

I thought dreams were entities bleeding vitality/But they're not what they seem/Some are self inflicted/Some restricted to change/Or rights to rearrange/Dark clouds into light/Plights for sleeping easy/Cheesy 'cause you lie awake at night/Flipping through comics about junkyard fights/The images slip from sheet to mind/And trying to unwind/Leads to a fist in a face being all you can find/Blind is what you've become/While trying to find/The divine line between happiness and emptiness/ And dream to be caressed by thoughts of hope instead of kids that cry/Why/Because dreams are like clouds/Because when dreams burst they burst with no control/I feel cold as shame dribbles on me/See the mistakes you've had to meet/But now you enter a world of imagination/Now I enter sleep

Reflected

Mirrors hold images

Reflect life while eyes and minds

Show true perfection

Turquoise Skies

Streams of turquoise

Gleam like dreams

You see in movie scenes

Apparent, but transparent

Not heard but still seen

It's in our genes

To lean

Back and track

Fluffy white sacks

Hanging from coat racks

But strength is what the racks lack

So the racks snap

And the sacks slap

Wasted, pasted to the dust

Leaving recent thoughts faded

And time underrated

So never fail to look to

Those streams of turquoise

That gleam like dreams you see

In movie scenes

And always stay true

To the life you lead

Guardians Among Us

Earth has it heroes

And so do we

They live among humans

Tending to most needs

Living creatures

We must respect

For they watch over all

But this we neglect

They take on the form

Of mammals we own

Even those freed

Small and fully grown

From the birds that oversee us

To the dogs that protect us

As they rest alert near our feet

To the cats that adore us

And the hamsters we keep for comfort

But my guardian does all of these

Although she is small

She is still strong

As all animals are

No matter to whom they belong

We owe these great creatures

Our lives and our souls

With their mounds of courage

And their strength so bold

Jacobi Copeland

Independent Independence

Cannon blasts from 1776

George sailing on Christmas Eve

Flag in a hand

Other hand leading troops

Long story short

Here we stand

Looking back

But not facing backwards

Looking up while looking down

Underground rests a brave one

Deceased but released from war

Served us even though

He does not know us

Showed us what we are capable of

And why we protect the very ground

Below us

Longed to find a free home

For us

Guided us across seas with his

Gentle ghost

To become freed from

Those who wished to dictate us

Looking back 237 years

Is why we add the blue and white

To the red of our blood

And mix the red and blue

With the white of our bones

But most of all

Keep those colors close

And paint your own portrait

Of gratitude

Jacobi Copeland

Barrier

Snap!

How's it look?

Crackle!

Is it pretty?

Boom!

It sounds great!

But if only images followed

Another year

Same place, same time

Where I live a life

Through all eyes but my own

I listen but not look

To the wonders that pass by

My soulless eyes

The shimmering blasts

Of color and light

Followed by mixtures of loud sound

And the soft "oohs and aahs"

Of watchers nearby

Someday it'll happen

Someday I'll break the barrier holding

Barrier molding my sight
To where nothing is seen
Someday it will all end
Someday the barrier will fall

Jacobi Copeland

Malagasy Blood

I'm one person
But I'm already divided
Between Spanish and Asian
All mixed and coated in a black shell
But I know where I come from
A small island below Africa's tip
Where my people live
Malagasy blood's
Running through my veins
No matter how vast time must travel
I'm a child of this island
Migrating up north
Down in Northern Spain
But that was centuries back
Until time caught up to me
Ever since I learned
My lineage is unique
My outlook has changed
But my heritage has not
That's a promise that will never
Be broken

Drawkcab

Taxi!

Take me to Albert St. on Jonas Blvd

No, I don't want a mint

I had a burger on the way

You know, I could really use some Parmesan crusted chicken

Yeah, isn't that at McDonald's?

No, I don't mean Olive Garden

They just have those yucky Fish McBites

No wait! You're about to pass it!

Ah man! Well, what else is up here?

Ooh, a movie theater!

I wanna go see Skies Dark!

I heard it got a Grammy for most uplifting film in the country!

Nooooo! You passed that too!

Whatever! Just take me to Jonas St on Albert Blvd.

No, not Albert on Jonas

Why do you say everything backwards?

Man, goodbye!

---Ring, Ring!

Hey, it's a call from my boss

Hello?

Yeah, I'm heading to work now

What?

Summer started today?

Guess there's only one thing to do

Taxi!

Jacobi Copeland

Infinity

Cities form a world

Worlds make up our universe

Until all restarts

Forecast Games

Rain drips from clouds fit to burst

Ready to play a game

It taps on our windows

But waits for none to take shelter

Rain will play dodgeball

And you'll always get caught

It beckons us out for a game of tag

 It seems like rain's always it

It cascades over our skin

Leaving it chilled but still inviting

Until the Sun breaks the tent

Of clouds to switch to a new game

High levels of heat tempt us

To play hide and seek

We all hide in our houses until

The sun gives up and goes away

The moon rises and pacifies the fun

As it lulls us all to sleep

Though we rest

The games never end

They happen over our heads

Without us even knowing it

Birds Underwater

There's a lake down the forest

That's causing a scene

Said a dirt poor farmer

In a V-neck and jeans

He's squawk his little tale

To all who would listen

After a gigantic bite

Outta his used-to-be fried chicken

I never believed

In that crazy old bat

Cause all used to know

That his lies were fat

So to prove what nonsense

This really is

Imma go to that lake

And be known as a wiz

Everyone'll be screaming

"We do believe you!"

While the hermit sits aside

Washed up and confused

But that couldn't happen

Till I've witnessed the thing
So I started for the lake
And began to sing:
"Folk stories be foolish
Folk stories be foolish
Old man be a fool
Cause folk stories be rubbish"
I decided to take a dive
As I got to the lake
So I pounced on that water
Just like a snake
I looked around
Not expecting a thing
But as I began to resurface
I heard something sing
Then I got the biggest
Scare of my life
I saw a bird behind me
Beak sharp as a knife
What's worse is that I noticed
That the bird was tweeting
It's beak was moving fast
As if it was eating
I swam away
As fast as I could

But more of them were coming

So that wasn't good

I kept on swimming

But I was running out of air

But I crawled to the lush shore

Gulping for air

So the hermit was right

And I tried to drown his voice

Which makes me feel awful

Cause that voice was God's choice

And when God made that choice

He wasn't just picking

So the very next day

I bought him some fried chicken

Jacobi became interested in writing when he was in 4th grade. He wrote his first story as an assignment for his 4th grade teacher, Ms. Grubbs. It told the story of an unusual family of five that travel to Las Vegas, Nevada and are pursued by a dangerously insane hotel worker. Jacobi's art teacher, Ms. Macintosh took a distinct interest in Jacobi's work and encouraged him to write more stories and poems, which fueled Jacobi's interest in writing. Jacobi is a huge fan of Star Wars, so he likes to base some of his work on science fiction, but he also enjoys writing poems that inspire and entertain.

Jacobi is particularly motivated by the poetry of Shel Silverstein, whom he pays tribute to in his poem, "Drawkcab." He and his family love to travel to different places in and out of the country and make their home in an Atlanta community where everyone looks out for one another.

Photo credit: arauzingink

VERBALEYZE
Press

Empowering young writers to say, **"I am my scholarship!"**

Open call for submissions to the *Young Writers Anthology*!

See your work in print!

Become a published writer!

**Earn royalites that can help
you pay for college!s**

VerbalEyze Press is accepting submissions from young adult writers, ages 13 to 22, in any of the following genres:

- poetry
- short story
- songwriting
- playwriting
- graphic novel
- creative non-fiction

For submission details, visit
www.verbaleyze.org

VerbalEyze serves to foster, promote and support the development and professional growth of emerging young writers.

Writers Cooperative

VerbalEyze is a nonprofit organization whose mission is to foster, promote and support the development and professional growth of emerging young writers.

The *Young Writers Anthology* is published as a service of VerbalEyze in furtherance of its goal to provide young writers with access to publishing opportunities that they otherwise would not have.

Fifty percent of the proceeds received from the sale of the *Young Writers Anthology* are paid to the authors in the form of scholarships to help them advance in their post-secondary education.

For more information about VerbalEyze and how you can become involved in its work with young writers, visit www.verbaleyze.org.